D1528361

NBA Teams

ATLANTA HAWKS

JOSH ANDERSON AND SAMANTHA NUGENT

AV2

www.openlightbox.com

Step 1
Go to **www.openlightbox.com**

Step 2
Enter this unique code

WOHAYU05M

Step 3
Explore your interactive eBook!

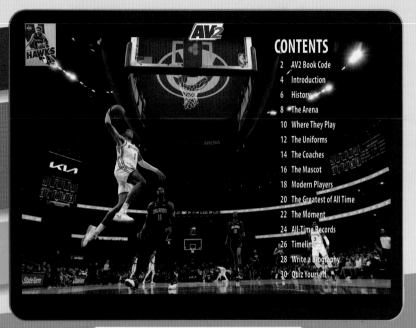

CONTENTS

AV2 is optimized for use on any device

Your interactive eBook comes with...

Contents
Browse a live contents page to easily navigate through resources

Audio
Listen to sections of the book read aloud

Videos
Watch informative video clips

Weblinks
Gain additional information for research

Slideshows
View images and captions

Try This!
Complete activities and hands-on experiments

Key Words
Study vocabulary, and complete a matching word activity

Quizzes
Test your knowledge

Share
Share titles within your Learning Management System (LMS) or Library Circulation System

Citation
Create bibliographical references following APA, CMOS, and MLA styles

This title is part of our AV2 digital subscription

1-Year Grades K–5 Subscription
ISBN 978-1-7911-3320-7

Access hundreds of AV2 titles with our digital subscription.
Sign up for a FREE trial at **www.openlightbox.com/trial**

The digital components of this book are guaranteed to stay active for at least five years from the date of publication.

ATLANTA HAWKS

Contents

Atlanta Hawks

Arena State Farm Arena

Division Southeast Division (Eastern Conference)

Head Coach Quin Snyder

Location Atlanta, Georgia

NBA Championships 1

6 Retired Numbers

168 Playoff Victories

21 Hall of Famers

2,891 Regular Season Wins

INTRODUCTION

In recent years, the Atlanta Hawks have built a team that has what it takes to make it to the National Basketball Association (NBA) Championship. Although the Hawks are good, they are working toward being great. The team has youth and talent, and now they need success.

The Hawks made the **playoffs** in back-to-back years during the 2020–21 and 2021–22 seasons. They almost made the NBA Finals during the 2020–21 season, when the team lost to the Milwaukee Bucks in the Eastern **Conference** Finals. It was the team's first visit to the conference finals since 2015.

The Atlanta Hawks have provided plenty of excitement on the court in recent years, and fans are hungry for an NBA title. After coming close to a championship several times, the Hawks are a team that is determined to win.

Point guard Dejounte Murray had 13 triple-doubles in the 2021–22 season. That means he had double-digits in three different statistical categories.

The Hawks won 41 games during the 2022–23 season.

History

First known as the Tri-Cities Blackhawks, the Hawks were one of the NBA's original **franchises** when the league began play in 1949. The Tri-Cities included the towns of Moline and Rock Island, Illinois, and Davenport, Iowa. The team moved to Milwaukee, Wisconsin, in 1951. Four years later, it moved to St. Louis, Missouri, and shortened its name to the St. Louis Hawks. During the team's time in St. Louis, the Hawks won their only NBA Championship. The franchise was in St. Louis from 1955 to 1968.

The team moved to Atlanta, Georgia, for the 1968–69 season. Hawks fans have enjoyed many trips to the playoffs, and a close-up look at one of the most exciting players in NBA history. Dominique Wilkins was a player so skilled at slam-dunking that he earned the nickname "The Human Highlight Film." Wilkins led the Hawks to the playoffs eight times and played in nine NBA **All-Star** Games.

From 2007–08 to 2016–17, the Hawks were very successful. They made the playoffs for 10 straight years. After missing the playoffs for three seasons in a row, the Hawks returned to the playoffs in both the 2020–21 and 2021–22 seasons.

🏀 In his first year as coach, Lenny Wilkens tied the team's regular season win record, with 57, and was named Coach of the Year.

The Arena

The first home of the Hawks, known then as the Tri-Cities Blackhawks, was Wharton Field House in Moline, Illinois. The team played there from 1946 until the move to Milwaukee in 1951. The new 10,000-seat Milwaukee Arena hosted the team until 1955. The Hawks' home in St. Louis, Missouri, was Keil Auditorium. The team played there until 1968, when it moved to Atlanta.

Prior to 1997, the Atlanta Hawks played most of their home games downtown at the Omni, which could seat more than 16,000 people. After the Omni was demolished in 1997, the team spent two seasons in temporary homes. The Hawks' permanent arena was completed in 1999.

The Hawks now play all of their home games at State Farm Arena, a state-of-the-art building located in the heart of Atlanta's downtown area. The arena's entryway greets visitors from all over the world with 65-foot-high (19.8-meters-high) steel columns. The record for attendance at a Hawks game in State Farm Arena was set on May 2, 2008. A crowd of 20,425 watched the Hawks defeat the Boston Celtics in game 6 of the first-round playoffs.

State Farm Arena is home not only to the Atlanta Hawks, but also to the Women's National Basketball Association's Atlanta Dream.

State Farm Arena, also known as the Highlight Factory, cost $213.5 million to build.

Where They Play

British
Columbia

Alberta

Saskatchewan

Manitoba

CANADA

Ontario

Washington

Montana

North Dakota

Minnesota

⑦

Wisconsin

㉕

⑨

Oregon

Idaho

⑩

South Dakota

Iowa

㉑

Illinois

⑤

Wyoming

Nebraska

Nevada

UNITED

STATES

①

Utah

Colorado

⑥

Kansas

Missouri

California

②

⑬

③

Arizona

④

New Mexico

⑧

Oklahoma

Arkansas

Mississ

Pacific
Ocean

MEXICO

⑪

Texas

⑮

Louisiana

⑫

Gulf of
Mexico

PACIFIC DIVISION
1. Golden State Warriors
2. Los Angeles Clippers
3. Los Angeles Lakers
4. Phoenix Suns
5. Sacramento Kings

NORTHWEST DIVISION
6. Denver Nuggets
7. Minnesota Timberwolves
8. Oklahoma City Thunder
9. Portland Trail Blazers
10. Utah Jazz

SOUTHWEST DIVISION
11. Dallas Mavericks
12. Houston Rockets
13. Memphis Grizzlies
14. New Orleans Pelicans
15. San Antonio Spurs

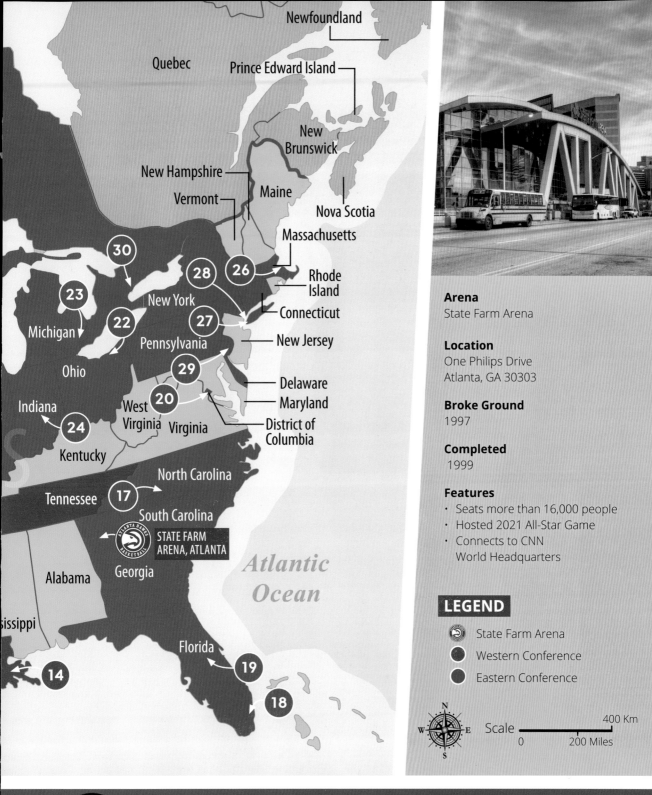

Map Labels

Newfoundland

Quebec

Prince Edward Island

New Brunswick

New Hampshire

Vermont

Maine

Nova Scotia

Massachusetts

Rhode Island

Connecticut

New York

New Jersey

Pennsylvania

Delaware

Maryland

District of Columbia

Michigan

Ohio

West Virginia

Virginia

Indiana

Kentucky

North Carolina

Tennessee

South Carolina

STATE FARM ARENA, ATLANTA

Alabama

Georgia

Atlantic Ocean

Mississippi

Florida

Arena
State Farm Arena

Location
One Philips Drive
Atlanta, GA 30303

Broke Ground
1997

Completed
1999

Features
- Seats more than 16,000 people
- Hosted 2021 All-Star Game
- Connects to CNN World Headquarters

LEGEND

- State Farm Arena
- Western Conference
- Eastern Conference

Scale

400 Km

0   200 Miles

NBA EASTERN CONFERENCE

SOUTHEAST DIVISION
16. Atlanta Hawks
17. Charlotte Hornets
18. Miami Heat
19. Orlando Magic
20. Washington Wizards

CENTRAL DIVISION
21. Chicago Bulls
22. Cleveland Cavaliers
23. Detroit Pistons
24. Indiana Pacers
25. Milwaukee Bucks

ATLANTIC DIVISION
26. Boston Celtics
27. Brooklyn Nets
28. New York Knicks
29. Philadelphia 76ers
30. Toronto Raptors

The Uniforms

The first Hawks uniforms were a combination of red and white. The team went back and forth for many years between having "Hawks" and "Atlanta" written across the chest of their jerseys. In other years, their home city's name was written on the front. The team colors were switched to blue and green for two seasons, from 1971 to 1972. The team then introduced a red and white uniform with pinstriped piping on the jersey and shorts. In 1976, the "Pac-Man" **logo** was added to the shorts, where it remained for most of the next two decades.

During the late 1990s, the team incorporated black into its main uniform design. A large image of a hawk was also added. For several years, the Hawks used navy blue in their uniform design.

The team currently has three different uniforms. The Icon Edition is white with yellow and red accents. The Statement Edition is black with yellow and red accents. The team also has a City Edition jersey, which is bright red with yellow and white accents.

CITY Edition

Quin Snyder played college basketball for the Duke University Blue Devils before becoming a coach. He worked as an assistant coach for nine different teams before taking over in Atlanta.

The Coaches

When the league named its Top 10 Coaches in NBA History, three were former coaches of the Hawks. Lenny Wilkens was the only one who had a winning record during his time with the team. The Hawks have been a training ground for some of the most successful NBA coaches of all time. Today, the focus of the entire Atlanta coaching staff is to reach the championships again.

RICHIE GUERIN

Richie Guerin's 327 victories as the head coach of the Hawks are the most in team history. During the 1960s and 1970s, he led the team to the postseason eight times. He owns the franchise record for most playoff victories, with 26. Guerin also played for the team during some of the seasons he coached the Hawks.

Regular Season Games

53%
327 Wins
291 Losses
47%

Playoff Games

39%
12 Wins
19 Losses
61%

LENNY WILKENS

After playing for the team for eight seasons in the 1960s, Wilkens returned to coach the Hawks during the 1990s. During his seven years as coach, the team made the playoffs six times. This Hall of Famer was the league's Coach of the Year in 1994 and coached Team USA to the gold medal at the 1996 Summer Olympic Games.

Regular Season Games

57%
310 Wins
232 Losses
43%

Playoff Games

36%
17 Wins
30 Losses
64%

QUIN SNYDER

Quin Snyder was the coach of the University of Missouri Tigers men's basketball team from 1999 to 2006. He led the Tigers to four appearances in a row in the NCAA Tournament and to the Elite Eight in 2002. From 2014 to 2022, Snyder coached the NBA's Utah Jazz. During that time, the Jazz made the playoffs six times. Snyder was hired as the Hawks, coach late in the 2022–23 season.

(As of 2022–23 season)

Regular Season Games

46%
13 Wins
15 Losses
54%

Playoff Games

33%
2 Wins
4 Losses
67%

The Mascot

Harry the Hawk has been entertaining fans at Hawks games since 1986. Until 2013, Harry's partner was the high-flying, slam-dunking Skyhawk. Since Skyhawk's retirement, Harry and the Hawks Cheerleaders have been on their own during halftime. Harry is easily spotted with his huge, red head and intimidating yellow beak. He wears a number 1 Hawks jersey.

When he is not entertaining the crowd at Hawks games, Harry the Hawk is usually out doing good in the community. Harry makes many appearances each year at schools and charitable functions. In 2023, Harry appeared with some of his mascot friends at the NBA All-Star Game. Harry is the second-highest paid mascot in the NBA.

Hawks Facts

Harry is best known for his **halfcourt shots** and **sledding** down the arena stairs.

Harry stands more than **6 feet (182.9 centimeters)** tall.

MODERN PLAYERS

Trae Young

Trae Young was drafted fifth overall in the 2018 **NBA Draft**. Scoring more than 19 points per game that year, he earned a spot on the 2018–19 All-Rookie Team. In 2021, Young helped lead the Hawks to the Eastern Conference Finals by averaging 25.3 points per game and 9.4 **assists** per game. In 2021–22, he led the NBA in total points, with 2,155, and total assists, with 737. One of the top long-range shooters in the game, Young has been chosen twice as an NBA All-Star.

Position: Point Guard
NBA Seasons: 2018–Present
Born: September 19, 1998, Lubbock, Texas, United States

Dejounte Murray

Dejounte Murray spent his first five NBA seasons playing for the San Antonio Spurs. He was chosen for the All-Star Game for the first time during his last season in San Antonio. During that season, he averaged 21.1 points per game and led the league with two **steals** per game. Murray joined the Hawks before the 2022–23 season, forming a strong backcourt with teammate Trae Young. Murray has finished in the top 10 in steals four times in his career, including his first season with Atlanta.

Position: Guard
NBA Seasons: 2016–Present
Born: September 19, 1996, Seattle, Washington, United States

De'Andre Hunter

De'Andre Hunter helped the University of Virginia win the team's first NCAA Championship in 2019. He scored his career-high 27 points in the final game of the tournament. That year, the National Association of Basketball Coaches named him college basketball's Defensive Player of the Year. Hunter joined the Hawks in 2019 and, in his first four seasons with the team, he averaged more than 13 points per game. Hunter had his highest scoring game as a professional in 2021 against the Milwaukee Bucks. Although the Hawks lost 129–115, he scored 33 points.

Position: Small Forward
NBA Seasons: 2019–Present
Born: December 2, 1997, Philadelphia, Pennsylvania, United States

John Collins

After playing two seasons at Wake Forest University, John Collins was picked by the Hawks in the first round of the 2017 NBA Draft. He earned a spot on the NBA's All-Rookie Second Team in 2018. Collins became the team's regular starting power forward during the 2018–19 season. He had his best season as a pro in 2019–20 when he averaged 21.6 points and 10.1 rebounds per game. Collins finished eighth in the league that season with a **field goal** percentage of 58.3. He has averaged nearly 16 points and 8 **rebounds** per game in his career so far.

Position: Power Forward
NBA Seasons: 2017–Present
Born: September 23, 1997, Layton, Utah, United States

THE GREATEST

There are several standout players on the Hawks roster who have worked hard to push the team to success. Often, there is one player who has become known as the "Greatest of All Time," or GOAT. This player has gone above and beyond to achieve greatness and to help his team shine.

Few players were as exciting to watch as Dominique "Nique" Wilkins. The two-time NBA Slam Dunk Champion was one of the greatest scorers in the history of the league. Wilkins is the Hawks' all-time leading scorer, finishing his Hawks career with 23,292 points. He is also the 15th-highest scorer in NBA history and led the league with 30.3 points per game in the 1985–86 season.

The nine-time NBA All-Star led the Hawks to four consecutive 50-win seasons in the late 1980s. He helped lead the Hawks to the postseason eight times. Twice, Wilkins scored 57 points in a single game, tying the team record. Wilkins played 12 seasons with the Hawks. He currently serves as Hawks VP of Basketball Operations.

DOMINIQUE WILKINS

Position • Small Forward

Seasons • 15 (1982–1999)

Born • January 12, 1960, Paris, France

OF ALL TIME

During his career with the Hawks, Wilkins made 8,752 field goals.

In his entire career, Wilkins came down with 2,950 offensive rebounds.

In 2015, Atlanta unveiled a statue of Wilkins, commemorating his legendary career with the team.

The Numbers

Wilkins played 7 games with **50 or more points** scored during his NBA career.

Dominque Wilkins scored **500 three pointers** with Atlanta.

Dominique Wilkins's career playoff **scoring average was 25.4**, which is the **20th best** in NBA history.

Wilkins played **882 games** for the Hawks.

The Moment

Entering the 2015 season, the Hawks had not reached the conference finals since 1970. If the team defeated the Washington Wizards in game 6 of the Eastern Conference Semifinals, they would advance to the second round of the playoffs. This game was played in the Verizon Center in Washington, DC.

The Hawks trailed at the end of the first quarter, 20–19. The second quarter featured five lead changes. Paul Millsap led the Hawks with 10 points in the quarter, including a shot with a second left in the half to put the Hawks ahead 45–39. The Hawks built their lead to 8 points, 72–64, by the end of the third, with DeMarre Carroll scoring 13 points in the quarter.

The Wizards' Bradley Beal led a comeback, as Washington took an 88–87 lead with just under four minutes left. Two minutes later, Millsap's jump shot gave the Hawks the lead. Seconds later, the Wizards tied the game 89–89. Finally, two baskets scored by DeMarre Carroll in the final minute put the Hawks ahead. Atlanta won 94–91.

🏀 Paul Millsap made Atlanta's third-highest number of field goal attempts, with 86, while playing against the Washington Wizards.

🏀 Mike Muscala only scored 12 points for the Hawks in the semifinals against the Washington Wizards, but he brought energy to the court and to the fans whenever he played.

ALL-TIME RECORDS

Most Three Pointers in a Season

Trae Young set the team record for most in a season, with 233 in 2021–22.

All-Time Points Scored

Dominique Wilkins is the Hawks' all-time scoring leader, with 23,292.

All-Time Assists

Glenn "Doc" Rivers set the Hawks' career assists record, with 3,866 during his eight seasons with the team.

Highest Field-Goal Percentage in a Season

Clint Capela set the Hawks' single-season record for field goal percentage during the 2022–23 season, with .653.

All-Time Steals

Mookie Blaylock is the Hawks' all-time leader in steals, with 1,321.

Shots Blocked in a Single Game

Wayne "Tree" Rollins once blocked 12 shots in a game. This is the most in Hawks history.

TIMELINE

Throughout the team's history, the Hawks have had many memorable events that have become defining moments for the team and its fans.

1949

The Tri-Cities Blackhawks defeat the Denver Nuggets 93–85 in the first NBA game played at Wharton Field House in Moline, Illinois.

1951

The team changes its name to the "Hawks" and moves to Milwaukee.

1955

The Hawks move for the second time in only six years, this time to St. Louis, Missouri.

1958

The Hawks win the NBA Championship, defeating the Boston Celtics in six games.

1968

Atlanta Braves broadcaster Milo Hamilton announces during a baseball game that the St. Louis Hawks are moving to Atlanta. The Hawks become the first professional basketball team in the history of the city.

1980

Behind John Drew, Eddie Johnson, and Dan Roundfield, the Hawks finish 50–32, ending the season in first place for the first time in nine seasons.

1982

The Hawks trade two players to the Utah Jazz in exchange for Dominique Wilkins. Two months later, Wilkins scores 23 points in his NBA debut.

1997

In game 2 of the Eastern Conference Semifinals, the Hawks become the first team since 1995 to win an away playoff game at Chicago's United Center.

2005

Rookie Josh Smith becomes the third Atlanta Hawk to win the Slam Dunk Contest. He earns perfect 50-point scores on three of his four dunks.

2015

The Hawks defeat the Philadelphia 76ers 91–85 for their 19th win in a row, a franchise record.

2021

The Hawks make the Eastern Conference Finals for the second time in the team's history but lose to the Milwaukee Bucks in a six-game series.

The Future

With stars Trae Young and Dejounte Murray leading in the backcourt, the future is bright in Atlanta. New coach Quin Snyder will try to build from the team's 2023 first-round playoff loss. He has the talent on the roster to do so.

WRITE A BIOGRAPHY

Life Story

A person's life story can be the subject of a book. This kind of book is called a biography. Biographies often describe the lives of people who have achieved great success. These people may be alive today, or they may have lived many years ago. Reading a biography can help you learn more about a great person.

Get the Facts

Use this book, and research in the library and on the internet, to find out more about your favorite star. Learn as much about this player as you can. What position does he play? What are his statistics in important categories? Has he set any records? Also, be sure to write down key events in the person's life.

What was his childhood like? What has he accomplished off the court? Is there anything else that makes this person special or unusual?

Use the Concept Web

A concept web is a useful research tool. Read the questions in the concept web on the following page. Answer the questions in your notebook. Your answers will help you write a biography.

Concept Web

Childhood
- Where and when was this person born?
- Describe his or her parents, siblings, and friends.
- Did this person grow up in unusual circumstances?

Work and Preparation
- What was this person's education?
- What was his or her work experience?
- How does this person work?
- What is the process he or she uses?

Help and Obstacles
- Did this individual have a positive attitude?
- Did he or she receive help from others?
- Did this person have a mentor?
- Did this person face any hardships?
- If so, how were the hardships overcome?

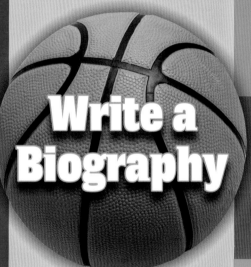

Write a Biography

Adulthood
- Where does this individual currently reside?
- Does he or she have a family?

Accomplishments on the Court
- What records does this person hold?
- What key moments have defined this person's career?
- What are the player's stats in key categories?

Your Opinion
- What did you learn from the books you read in your research?
- Would you suggest these books to others?
- Was anything missing from these books?

Accomplishments off the Court
- What is this person's life's work?
- Has he or she received awards or recognition for accomplishments?
- How have this person's accomplishments served others?

Key Words

All-Star: a mid-season game made up of the best-ranked players in the NBA. A player can be named an All-Star and then be sent to play in this game.

assists: a statistic that is attributed to up to two players of the scoring team who shoot, pass, or deflect the ball toward the scoring teammate

conference: an association of sports teams that play each other

field goal: a basket scored while the clock is running and the ball is in play

franchises: teams that are a member of a professional sports league

logo: a symbol that stands for a team or organization

NBA Draft: the annual event in June where NBA teams select players from college to join the league. Teams select in order based on the prior season's winning percentages.

playoffs: a series of games that occur after regular season play

rebounds: taking possession of the ball after missed shots

steals: taking possession of the ball from the other team

Index

Get the best of both worlds.

AV2 bridges the gap between print and digital.

The expandable resources toolbar enables quick access to content including **videos**, **audio**, **activities**, **weblinks**, **slideshows**, **quizzes**, and **key words**

Animated videos make static images come alive.

Resource icons on each page help readers to further **explore key concepts**.

Published by Lightbox Learning Inc.
276 5th Avenue, Suite 704 #917
New York, NY 10001
Website: www.openlightbox.com

Library of Congress Control Number: 2023940668

ISBN 978-1-7911-5340-3 (hardcover)
ISBN 978-1-7911-5341-0 (multi-user eBook)

Printed in Guangzhou, China
1 2 3 4 5 6 7 8 9 0   27 26 25 24 23

072023
101322

Project Coordinator John Willis
Art Director Terry Paulhus

Photo Credits
Every reasonable effort has been made to trace ownership and to obtain permission to reprint copyright material. The publisher would be pleased to have any errors or omissions brought to its attention so that they may be corrected in subsequent printings. The publisher acknowledges Alamy, Getty Images, and Newscom as its primary image suppliers for this title.